To Do Justice

A CHRISTIAN SOCIAL CONSCIENCE

Bernard Häring, C.SS.R.

LIGUORI CELEBRATION SERIES

Liguori

ONE LIGUORI DRIVE
LIGUORI MO 63057-9999
314.464.2500

Imprimi Potest:
Richard Thibodeau, C.Ss.R.
Provincial, Denver Province
The Redemptorists

Imprimatur:
Most Reverend Michael J. Sheridan
Auxiliary Bishop, Archdiocese of St. Louis

ISBN 0-7648-0466-9
Library of Congress Catalog Card Number: 99-71465

© 1999, Munich Province of the Redemptorists
Printed in the United States of America
03 02 01 00 99   5 4 3 2 1

Scripture quotations from the *New Revised Standard
Version of the Bible,* © 1989 by the Division of Christian
Education of the National Council of the Churches of Christ
in the USA. Used with permission. All rights reserved.

Quotations from Vatican II documents taken from *Vatican
Council II, the basic sixteen documents: Constitutions,
Decrees, Declarations. A completely revised translation in
inclusive language. Austin Flannery, OP, general editor,
© Costello Publishing Company: Northport, NY and
Dominican Publications: Dublin, Ireland (1996).*

Chapter page quotations from Bernard Haring, C.Ss.R., *The
Virtues of an Authentic Life: A Celebration of Spiritual
Maturity,* © Liguori Publications: Liguori, MO (1997).

This book is a revised edition of materials that originally
appeared in *Dare To Be Christian: Developing a Social
Conscience,* © 1983, Liguori Publications.

Cover design by Wendy Barnes

Table *of* Contents

Seek *the* Truth

The three dimensions of truthfulness (in thought, word, and deed) are comparable to…the fruitful, dynamic inter-existence of the three divine Persons…. The high point of truthfulness…is the joyful, loyal, and creative doing of the truth—the doing of which is a promise and a pointing to the eternal feast of the truth and truthfulness of love.

Pilate asked him, "So you are a king?"

Jesus answered, "You say that I am a king. For this I was born, and for this I came into the world, to testify to the truth. Everyone who belongs to the truth listens to my voice."

Pilate asked him, "What is truth?"

John 18:37-38a

Faced with the greatest decision in human history, Israel's ruling class and the representative of Roman world power are thoroughly immersed in the quest for earthly power. They see truth and justice only in the perspective of their own main interests. They are unwilling and, in a certain sense, already unable to deal directly with truth and justice. A truth that does not serve their interests leaves them skeptical. Even their religion is viewed as an instrument of power. Thus their access to saving truth is blocked, as is also the pathway to justice.

Today's world is in a situation similar to that of Pilate and the ruling class of Israel: Our interest in truth and our allegiance to it are dangerously off target.

The world needs people who seek truth, the ultimate meaning of life—saving truth. It needs people who pursue it in an honest exchange of genuine convictions in discussion with others.

Mature Christians know that Christ is *the Truth*. For them, the one thing that matters is to know Christ and, through him, the Father, thus coming to know ever better the origin, destiny, and vocation of God's people.

Before us stands the powerless witness of the saving truth, the Truth in person. Through this powerlessness shines the divine majesty of this central truth, incarnate in Jesus Christ who will seal it with his blood as Redeemer.

Facing the Divine Truth

The "I-am-the-Truth" of John's Gospel shows us that the vital decision of all humanity is made in confrontation with the truth for which we stand, for which we live and die. "Everyone who belongs to the truth listens to my voice" (John 18:37c).

When we face "I-am-the-Truth" and his authentic witnesses, there is no legitimate escape into mere theoretical questions. We all must make a decision about our own truth of existence; and, in doing so, we reveal either our adherence to truth or our alienation from it. Those who sincerely seek the saving truth and act accordingly are at home with the words of Jesus; they rejoice in hearing his voice. The fundamental option to seek ultimate truth and meaning and to act on them clears the way for the blessed reign of truth. This liberating experience of ever-new horizons of truth helps us better appreciate "I-am-the-Truth."

With all the ardor of his love and in full awareness of his being sent by the Father, Jesus speaks about this mystery of God and human:"This is eternal life, that they may know you, the only true God, and Jesus Christ whom you have sent" (John 17:3).

Exultingly, he announces the happiness of those who have entered into this realm of knowledge and truth. "The words that you gave to me I have given to them, and they have received them and know in truth that I came from you; and they have believed that you sent me" (John 17:8). At the same time, he prays fervently for his disciples, that they may loyally proclaim this truth to the world which so badly needs it."Sanctify them in the truth...that they may all be one. As you, Father, are in me and I am in you, may they also be in us, so that the world may believe that you have sent me" (John 17:17a, 21).

Attainment of this truth comes from the work of the Spirit of Truth. By their fundamental option, made with heart, mind, and will, the disciples of Christ open themselves to the promptings of the Holy Spirit.

I will ask the Father, and he will give you another Advocate, to be with you forever. This is the Spirit of truth, whom the world cannot receive, because it neither sees him nor knows him. You know him, because he abides with you, and he will be in you.

John 14:16-17

The "world" of which Jesus speaks is that of people locking themselves into their own pride, trusting in their own achievement. This is true of the people of today's world who seem unable to rise above the realm of experimental knowledge, of truth sought only for utility's sake.

Listening to the Spirit of Truth

"The Advocate, the Holy Spirit, whom the Father will send in my name, will teach you everything, and remind you of all that I have said to you" (John 14:26). The word "everything" in this quotation does not mean an encyclopedic knowledge, but rather an encompassing vision of reality in the light of Christ's Gospel. That is what the world of today so urgently needs.

Through Christ's faithful disciples who entrust themselves to the power of the Spirit of Truth, this very Spirit "will prove the world wrong about sin and righteousness and judgment" (John 16:8). Even those who rely only on their own strength will finally be able to see their error and alienation when faced with Christ's *true* disciples, who are determined to seek God's kingdom and are filled with joy, peace, and love. Those who seek only their own interests and power will come to realize how far they are from righteousness and truth. Their restless and ruthless search for more power, more possessions, more consumption will be seen—in very truth— as bringing misery to themselves and others while alienating them from saving and all-encompassing truth and justice (see John 16:8-13).

All people of good will can learn, from those who are guided by the Spirit of God, that they cannot dwell in the truth unless they effectively take sides with the unloved, the oppressed, the downtrodden.

Those who are on the pathway of truth will understand that, for their own salvation as well as for the sake of all of humankind, they still have to go a long way before they are completely transformed—in their whole being and all their relationships—by the truth. But grace calls to them and comes to them.

May grace and peace be yours in abundance in the knowledge of God and of Jesus our Lord. His divine power has given us everything needed for life and godliness, through the knowledge of him who called us by his own glory and goodness. Thus he has given us, through these things, his precious and very great promises, so that through them you may escape from the corruption that is in the world because of lust, and may become participants of the divine nature. For this very reason, you must make every effort to support your faith with goodness, and goodness with knowledge, and knowledge with self-control, and self-control with endurance, and endurance with godliness, and godliness with mutual affection, and mutual affection with love.

2 Peter 1:2-7

Our concern must be that our knowledge of our Lord Jesus Christ will not be useless or barren for the life of the world (see 2 Peter 1:8), but rather fruitful in truth and love. God is love, and we are to be God's image. Knowledge of salvation leads us on the pathway of love, and as we love better we are led to a deeper and more blessed knowledge of truth.

The Wisdom of Truth

The apostle of the Gentiles rejoices that he is privileged to impart not the wisdom of the rulers of his time but "God's wisdom, secret and hidden, which God decreed before the ages for our glory" (1 Corinthians 2:7).

While today's situation is in many ways different from that of Paul's time, it is an astounding and alarming sign of our times that the so-called "developed" world schools its people mainly in the area of acquiring material goods and in the exercise of domination, especially the practice of "right by might."

Structural changes are necessary, but they will not succeed without men and women outstanding in wisdom. Christians have to become more aware of what they can and must give to the world if they are to be faithful to their calling.

We have received not the spirit of the world, but the Spirit that is from God, so that we may understand the gifts bestowed on us by God. And we speak of these things in words not taught by human wisdom but taught by the Spirit, interpreting spiritual things to those who are spiritual.

1 Corinthians 2:12-13

The wisdom that concerns us is wisdom about the destiny and calling of men and women, understood in light of the love of the Creator and Redeemer. Vatican II speaks about this in regard to our vocation to holiness.

Christ, who died and was raised up for the sake of all, can show people the way and strengthen them through the Spirit so that they become worthy of their destiny: nor is there given any other name under heaven by which they can be saved. The church likewise believes the key, the center and the purpose of the whole of human history is to be found in its Lord and Master.

Gaudium et Spes, "The Church in the Modern World," 10

As Christians, we are open-minded to every kind of truth. We learn from humanity's historical experience made accessible to us through scientific research. We cannot ignore the natural sciences which unfold many secrets—processes that explain the give-and-take of the created world. They not only help us to admire God's wonderful work, but also are indispensable for human health, food production, and many other human needs. Nor can we ignore the behavioral sciences, which improve our understanding of human development, psychic growth, and social relationships.

Authentic Christians will be distinguished from the unbelieving and uninformed by their priorities and their vision of wholeness. Saving truth comes first: to know God and to know people in the light of Christ. And Christians should never forget that such knowledge cannot be acquired in the same ways as knowledge for material success and the exercise of domination. Since God is love, and since our vocation is to be and to become ever more an image of God, the genesis and progression on our pathway of truth depend on the firmness and depth of our fundamental option for redeemed and redeeming love.

This insight was sharply brought home to me by an experience in a leprosarium in India. There I met a young and gifted artist from Paris. When she, who had been brought up in total atheism, began to ask and discuss religious questions, a young man told her one day with astonishing conviction: "The God in whom we believe cannot be found by mere reasoning and discussion. Since God is Love, God can be found only by loving people."

She told us that those words affected her deeply. She kept asking herself: "But how can I be sure that what I intend to do is really done for love's sake?" She decided then, on the spur of the moment, to serve for one year in the rehabilitation of lepers in India, especially because of her terrible distaste for this kind of misery. At the end of the year, she chose to remain there, in gratitude to God and to these poor people, because they had helped her to find God—to find love.

Our Devotion to Truth

Our devotion to truth implies a wonderful wholeness which we describe as being truthful, thinking truthfully, and speaking and acting truthfully.

Being truthful

The world—deceived by so many ideologies, power structures, collective and individual egotisms—is in dire need of our being truthful, of our "being in the truth." We can dialogue as Christians only if we have found and are living our identity, our "yes" to the saving truth in Jesus Christ. To "be in the truth" implies an absolutely sincere conscience—a conscience formed in truthfulness to God and ourselves, matured in open discussion with others who seek the truth, and acted out in everyday affairs. Further, it implies fidelity, reliability, and total commitment to "act out the truth in love." This truthfulness and clarity of conscience coincide with "purity of heart," the purity of intentions and motives so highly praised in the Sermon on the Mount.

As pilgrims, we cannot "be in the truth" without humbly acknowledging that we are, at best, only on the road to greater fullness of truthfulness in being and in acting. This gives us the courage to confess our sins and shortcomings and to accept the need for further conversion to the One who can say, "I-am-the-Truth," while praising God constantly for having called us into divine light.

Thinking truthfully

People whose thinking has become superficial, confused, or even chaotic, can be helped greatly by contact with persons whose minds and hearts are filled with the exhilarating truth revealed in Jesus Christ. These persons give priority to salvation truth, and cultivate other forms of knowledge according to their scale of values and of service to love and justice. They take care to know God, to recognize Christ, to understand human dignity and destiny—all because of their love of truth. And, out of gratitude for their knowledge, they strive for ever deeper and more integrated knowledge. Those who want to think truthfully will also develop a contemplative dimension of human life, arranging for quiet times and being temperate in the search for news and information, discerning those things that are truly worth considering.

Speaking and acting truthfully

These go hand in hand. People's faces radiate either their purity of heart and mind, or they reveal their frustration, restlessness, hostility of thought and intention. Our actions are highly qualified communications. If they arise from our being in the truth and thinking the truth in love, they generate healthy relationships and build up the community in truth.

As Christians, we speak truth only insofar as we speak with authentic love and in the service of love and justice. Our truthful words and actions resemble the Word Incarnate who, from all eternity, is that Word which breathes love and sends us the Spirit of Truth, enabling us to act out the truth in love.

Whoever uses acquired knowledge to hurt or damage others is not in the truth, does not think truthfully, does not speak the truth. Abuse of information is allied to the work of the devil. The service of truth requires discretion, prudence, discernment. True disciples of Christ are discreet about what they say and to whom they say it (see Matthew 7:6).

Refusal to participate in the malice of others is a firm "yes" to our mission to be the "salt of the earth." This can be exemplified by the response of Christian nurses, during the reign of Hitler, to the hangmen who asked at their orphanage about the number of children under their care who were affected by hereditary diseases. What they were *really* asking was not about sick children in need of help, but simply about victims for the gas chambers and soap factories. The women's response to the *real* question could *only* be, "We have no such children." Holiness has nothing to do with naivety.

Prayer

Lord Jesus Christ, before your sacrificial death you prayed for us to the Father: "Sanctify them in the truth!" Send forth the Holy Spirit to lead us into a growing knowledge of your love and truth, a loving knowledge of the Father and a saving knowledge of ourselves and our brothers and sisters. Cleanse our hearts, our minds, our wills through the Spirit of Truth. Help us to strive toward an ever fuller knowledge of our faith and all that it implies. Gather us together in your name, so that we can assist each other in our love for truth and our joy in the saving truth.

Help us to rid ourselves of senseless curiosity about thousands of petty things, and teach us to ignore all news which contributes nothing to our growth or our mission and ministry. Assist and illumine us in our striving for whatever knowledge is necessary for skillful service to others.

Remind those who—with all their learning—seem to know nothing about justice, love, and salvation. They are blind and are ignorant of truth. Grant them hunger and thirst for the essential truths.

With you, Lord Jesus, we praise the Father for having revealed the secrets of salvation to the simple ones while they remain hidden from the arrogant who boast about their wisdom (see Luke 10:21). Through the power of the Spirit of Truth, help us to seek the truth honestly and sincerely. Teach us to learn from the humble and the poor.

Be Open *to* Dialogue

> **O**penness is an inestimable endowment that readies us for dialogue....When openness is coupled with alertness to the here and now and the gift of discernment, this union creates fruitful simultaneity, contemporaneousness, and a community marching toward the future. Open people discover and appreciate the opportunities of each moment.

Do not refrain from speaking at the proper moment, and do not hide your wisdom. For wisdom becomes known through speech, and education through the words of the tongue. Never speak against the truth, but be ashamed of your ignorance. Do not be ashamed to confess your sins, and do not try to stop the current of a river. Be quick to hear, but deliberate in answering. If you know what to say, answer your neighbor; but if not, put your hand over your mouth. Honor and dishonor come from speaking, and the tongue of mortals may be their downfall. Do not be called double-tongued and do not lay traps with your tongue; for shame comes to the thief, and severe condemnation to the double-tongued. Do not answer before you listen, and do not interrupt when another is speaking. Some people keep silent and are thought to be wise,

*while others are detested for being talkative. Some
people keep silent because they have nothing to say,
while others keep silent because they know when to
speak. The wise remain silent until the right moment,
but a boasting fool misses the right moment. Whoever
talks too much is detested, and whoever pretends to
authority is hated.*

Sirach 4:23-26;5:11-14;11:8;20:5-8

The art of dialogue plays a necessary role in securing
harmony on the path of truth. Sirach emphasizes especially the discernment of participants, the readiness to
listen and to learn, and the need for mutual support in
the search for wisdom.

There is an unchangeable relationship between our
dialogue with God and our dialogue with other human
persons. In communion with God, it is evident that the
first condition is to listen and to acknowledge God's initiative. God speaks to us through all of creation, through
the events of our lives and our times, and—in a special
way—through people who have opened themselves to
wisdom and kindness. Happy are those who live with
others, and who know how to listen to God and to make
all their life a response to God's Word.

Jesus Christ is not only the final and supreme Word
spoken to us by the Father; he is also the matchless master of dialogue. The incarnate Son lives wholly by the
word that comes from the Father. He is the perfect lis-
tener.

The Gospel shows us clearly how strikingly Jesus has
listened to the words of God in Scripture, but equally
how attentively he listens to the wise, to people's needs,
and to the cry of the downtrodden and the sinners.

Jesus, the teacher, dialogues with his friends and also with his enemies. By listening, he receives the information he wants. He asks questions and responds to questions. Through dialogue, he learns what others are experiencing, what problems they are facing. Then he leads them patiently to a deeper vision. What a wonderful example is his dialogue with the woman of Samaria (see John, chapter 4).

Dialogue is a basic human experience. It becomes an excellent form of human art when people not only speak words with each other but also express themselves in openness and trust, manifesting their love and assuring each other of their fidelity.

Dialogue in Our World

Partners gifted with the art of dialogue do not pick words apart. Neither do they just listen to words. They meet their partners as unique persons, with an intuitive sense of the kindness, happiness, sympathy, trouble, or pain that underlies the other's words and gestures.

In its full sense, dialogue is sharing joy and sorrow with the other; it is grateful reception and enrichment, not only of knowledge and experience, but also of learning to love better, with greater sympathy and reverence, and thus to discover each other's inner being and resources.

The effect of dialogue depends on both its content and the way it is conducted. A marriage or friendship gains much if there is a sharing of high ideals, vital interests, commitment to an important cause, and a continuing search for deeper knowledge of truth and wisdom.

Children can help us to progress in the art of dialogue, to understand what Jesus meant when he invited us to become like children: single-minded, cordial, open.

Children experience great encouragement when their first efforts to talk are taken seriously and are a source of joy for the family.

Happy are the children whose parents and educators are willing and able to listen to the children in their uniqueness, in their joys and in their needs, and to speak with them in such a way that they can better discover their capabilities and meet their difficulties.

If parents and teachers are competent partners in dialogue, children will express themselves confidently in conversation and questions. When parents acknowledge that they do not know the right answer to a question and need time to check it out, children begin to learn an important aspect of good dialogue. And it is even more fruitful when an adult acknowledges, with truthful simplicity: "I was wrong; I should not have said (or done) that; I am sorry."

Not the least of dialogue's riches are sharing joys with another and being open to various forms of enjoyment. For this, a sense of humor is a marvelous charism. Even in a time of sadness, the conversation can be lightened with moments of cheer, of hope, of happy or humorous reminiscences.

Sirach calls our attention to the art of listening, of silence—alertness for the right moment and the right word. To learn all this takes time and patience. We have to examine the quality of our dialogue again and again in order to improve it. It is helpful, sometimes even necessary, to dialogue deeply about the meaning, purpose, and quality of our day-by-day communication.

Dialogue is an expression of our complementarity. In mature dialogue, we acknowledge the other as other, grateful that he or she is different from us. It can be only be enriching if both affirm their equal dignity and rejoice in their diversity.

Dialogue between and among all concerned parties is the proper way to arrive at decisions. One of the greatest evils in today's world is the arrogance of those who set themselves up as sole arbiters of matters that deeply affect the lives of others. Decisions would be more just and prudent if all concerned were allowed to contribute their skills, experiences, viewpoints, and interests. It would then also be easier to put decisions into practice.

Dialogue with the World

To share or communicate faith by witness and word is one of the noblest forms of dialogue. At the heart of this dialogue lies our common effort to discern events and experiences in the light of faith. In this way, we share the joy of faith and the consolation that both comes from God and leads to God.

The dialogue of faith becomes perfect when participants are aware that they are gathered in the name of the Lord who is present with them. Ideal friendship is anchored in this friendship with the Lord. Dialogue between believing friends arises from and leads to intimate dialogue with the Lord.

Paul's first letters (especially 1 Corinthians 14) show us how spontaneous and dynamic the dialogue of faith was in that early community. Because of these characteristics, efforts had to be made to keep it on a high level, and at the same time to guarantee a minimum of order. The saint's letters indicate also that, in the dialogue of faith, a great diversity of charisms and experiences are included. Belief that this diversity enriches dialogue and unity is grounded in the truth that the *one* Spirit builds up unity through the very diversity of gifts and ministries, since each charism is given by the Spirit for the benefit of all.

If then there is any encouragement in Christ, any consolation from love, any sharing in the Spirit, any compassion and sympathy, make my joy complete: be of the same mind, having the same love, being in full accord and of one mind. Do nothing from selfish ambition or conceit, but in humility regard others as better than yourselves. Let each of you look not to your own interests, but to the interests of others.

Philippians 2:1-4

What Paul prescribes for individuals is also true for the entire Church. Those in authority depend greatly upon the manifold charisms and particular skills available among the people of God. All this needs encouragement, and the kind of channeling that favors creativity and produces results for the benefit of all.

The basic principles of collegiality and subsidiarity point in this direction. In the worldwide Church there must be ample room, even on the institutional level, for dialogue among the various cultures, historical experiences, traditions, customs, skills, and needs. A fanaticism for uniformity is an impoverishment, and an enemy of love and mutual appreciation.

If the Church, in its inner life, shows itself as a model of fostering and articulating dialogue on all levels, it can also make a most valuable contribution to the promotion of dialogue within the secular world, even among the various ideologies and world views. No one can doubt that the art of dialogue is a basic premise for all endeavors to bring about peace and justice.

Prayer

Lord, how exciting it is to know that all of your creation and all the events of redemption originated in a dialogue with us. You made us capable of listening, and you assure us that you are interested in our response. In all our needs, as well as in our joys, we are encouraged to speak to you with gratitude and confidence.

Lord, teach us how to be silent before you in order to understand better your message. Speak to our hearts as well as to our minds. Move our wills, so that we can entrust ourselves to you and always search earnestly to understand your design for us.

We thank you, loving God, for the gift of speech and language, for ears and tongue. We thank you for all the loving people who share with us, not only their knowledge but also the art of loving, the art of listening, to console and to encourage.

Lord, send forth your Spirit to teach us to remain open to that dialogue which makes each one of us an image and likeness of your triune life, of your loving presence among us. Teach us the kind of prayer that nourishes fruitful human dialogue, responds to your initiative, and foreshadows the divine dialogue of heaven. We praise forever your bounty, which invites us even now to be adorers of your divine life in word and love.

Harmonize Labor
with Leisure

U nless we bring some standards of evaluation
to all our desires and to our whole lifestyle,
we can never grow in the love of God and our
neighbor....We rejoice in God's splendid creation.
The whole work of Redemption calls out to us:
"Rejoice in the Lord at all times."

---

*I was glad when they said to me, "Let us go to the
house of the LORD!"*

Our feet are standing within your gates, O Jerusalem.

*Jerusalem—built as a city that is bound firmly
together. To it the tribes go up, the tribes of the LORD, as
was decreed for Israel, to give thanks to the name of
the LORD. For there the thrones for judgment were set
up, the thrones of the house of David.*

*Pray for the peace of Jerusalem: "May they prosper
who love you. Peace be within your walls, and security
within your towers."*

*For the sake of my relatives and friends I will say,
"Peace be within you."*

*For the sake of the house of the LORD our God, I will
seek your good.*

Psalm 122

The ultimate meaning of life lies neither in work nor in play. A fulfilled life implies both meaningful leisure and honorable, socially relevant work. In the biblical sense, life is a feast manifesting its meaning and joy in all of life's dimensions.

Jesus has not only labored in our behalf and borne the burden of the cross; we know him equally as the one who concelebrates the feasts of Israel, sings the joyful songs of the pilgrims on their way to the house of God. He exults in his work and his praise of his Father. These are his resources, giving him the strength to carry his cross. Before going to his death, Jesus institutes the Eucharist which both anticipates and leads us to the heavenly banquet of eternal bliss.

Christians are set free for joyous festival: for dancing before the Lord, quiet contemplation, raptures of love, conviviality, laughter flowing from a liberating sense of humor. Festive and leisure times constitute our relaxed but firm "yes" to life's meaning: occasions for sharing life's joys, for strengthening solidarity in both joy and sorrow, and for developing creativity. This has great impact on our personal growth, creative liberty, and fidelity.

A Sense of Celebration

When we celebrate feast days and make our life festive in expectation of the eternal feast, we know that life is good and has an ultimate purpose beyond all the purposes of organized work. We have reason for contemplation and celebration. We are constantly invited to rejoice in all that is good, true, and beautiful; to recall our roots in God who *is* love, goodness, truth, beauty.

Quite different are the festive occasions and leisure times of persons driven by the anguish of not being able to amass enough material goods to satisfy themselves. The prophet gives us a sad picture of them: "Let us eat and drink, for tomorrow we die" (Isaiah 22:13). These try to still the outcry of the poor and the cry of their own hearts, which yearn for ultimate meaning, true love, and joy. They hope that incessant noise will deafen them to their inner voice, which calls for conversion.

Even more deplorable are the "festivals" of dictators whose ideologies call for a class struggle to free the masses; who, in their lust for power, deadly bureaucracy, and murderous arms race, have already buried even the false hopes of their original ideology. They feast on the great parades of their newest weaponry and the applause of their propagandized masses.

Leisure, festive celebration, play, and dance mean more than repose from work and restoration of strength for work. They bear meaning in themselves for all who are searching for life's final meaning. They are gateways to new horizons.

The Book of Genesis helps us to discover the meaning of Sabbath in view of the supreme dignity of humankind, created in God's own image. The seventh day should remind God's people not only of the Creator's works, but also of the Creator's repose: God's celebration of love and joy over and above all God's creative works (see Genesis 1:27; 2:1-4).

God does not want us to be drudges, slaves of work. The holy days, guaranteeing repose and leisure, are meant to help us develop our noblest capacities for worship, for joy, and for love. Only thus can we be faithful and creative stewards of the earth entrusted to us. We cannot be true images of God in work unless we first of all image God in the festive joy that calls for love and unity.

Jesus insists that the Sabbath is for people (see Mark 2:27). It is a privilege, an invitation to a supreme sharing in God's feast day of peace. But it is also a fundamental social rule to protect servants, migrants, slaves (see Exodus 20:10). It reminds us that, before God, the poor and oppressed are of the same dignity as the rich and powerful; that none may celebrate the feast of liberation wrought by God while refusing a share in the benefits to others who are weaker. The world needs saints who celebrate life in God's way: as a feast to which all others are invited.

Joy in the Liturgy

Our Christian life is marked by the annual liturgical cycle, which offers a sharing in salvation history through grateful remembrance of God's wonderful deeds of creation and redemption, the expectation of an eternal sharing in God's glory and bliss, and the ongoing discovery of present opportunities.

Those who truly celebrate the feasts of salvation are encouraged, not only to deal with their own troubles but also to bear the burdens of others. They know well that only in this way will they celebrate with all those of good will the feast of eternal life.

The Eucharist, sacrifice and banquet, memorial and pledge of abiding hope, opens our eyes to the abyss of sin in the light of Christ's cross while also assuring us of the final victory of justice and love. Our celebration of the remembrance and hope of liberation, and of the presence of God who is the helper of the poor, is sincere and productive only if we unite with others in the struggle for the dignity and liberty of all people.

There are some who deny themselves the very inner resources of peace, without which they cannot prevent discord, hatred, or injustice. If we refuse to take time to adore God in community and welcome the Good News, we miss the chance to exorcise false gods from our own hearts and dangerous idols from public life.

The Christian feast days, and the regular observance of Sunday that repeatedly celebrates the Easter event, are amazing gifts from the Lord of salvation history. The liturgical calendar is a teaching masterpiece; we would not be so restless and unstable if we would thankfully accept this divine pedagogy.

This is not to imply that the celebrations of the Church claim a kind of monopoly. Still, their centrality touches on all the joys and sorrows of life while yet leaving room for our multiple forms of festivity and recreation. And everything that is genuine in the festive celebrations of families, neighborhoods, and cultures can serve as a prelude to religious celebrations.

Dance and play is indispensable in human culture. Children need play, playmates, and joy in play. Parents who play with their children reap their own joyous harvest of serenity. Delight in play and regard for rules of fair play prevent a too heavy seriousness, and allow participants to work together as a team in preparation for future tasks in life. On the way to the eternal feast in the glory of God, we are team players, "members of the cast" in the play of redemption, of the gradual breakthrough of joy and love.

Surely, we also need purposefulness in our life, a prudent coordination of means (tools and methods) and ends (goals). But goals and tools must not be allowed to dominate us. God offers us many joys without subordinating them in any way to direct purposes. We should habitually accept the invitation simply to rejoice, to sing, and to play!

A Sense of Humor

Throughout history, artists have portrayed human beings as echoes of God's own rejoicing. Christians who know that they are redeemed can laugh in spite of their problems and their suffering, for they believe that the last word in history is the victory of love and joy.

All are not especially gifted with a sense of humor, but no saint will ever disdain this wonderful gift. It is, indeed, a priceless charism that often provides proper perspective for the discussion at hand and opens our eyes to a more balanced vision of what is happening. It can be a marvelous peacemaking charism. As Christians, we recognize the world's natural inclination to evil; we know about folly and sin. But we also know that, after all, victory lies in plentiful redemption. So we allow ourselves and others a touch of levity while constantly striving for greater wisdom.

A genuine and healthy sense of humor never focuses on other people's faults or foibles. The tone and target of our humor should rest on the constant awareness that we too have our faults. We all need the therapy that humor provides.

Christian humor has its roots in the knowledge that, in spite of our sins and shortcomings, we are accepted and reconciled by God. An uplifting and agreeable sense of humor is a concrete sign and symbol of faith that conquers the hearts of many. It originates, not from superficial or blind optimism, but from actual contact with God's graciousness, which allows us to discover a reason for wit and laughter where others see only doom. It signals hope and redeemed freedom.

Prayer

We thank you, God, that you grant us time to rest after all our toil, and festive joy and leisure for contemplation. Like children, we can play before you, confident that it pleases you to see us bring happiness to each other by playing together and celebrating in community.

We thank you for the great feast days of the Church in which we can experience saving solidarity and shared joy. Through them, you remind us of our past salvation history and direct our eyes and steps toward the eternal homeland. You help us discover the richness of the present moment, reassuring us of your abiding presence and loving care.

We thank you, Lord, for yearly remembrances of our birthday and our day of baptism. You have called us into being, given us a unique name, and assumed us into the family of the redeemed.

Thank you for all our family feasts and celebrations, for play and song with brothers and sisters, for the time our parents took to play and to talk with us.

Thank you for the wonderful people who, through wit and humor, have helped us to see redemption at work and to discover essential dimensions of life, of beauty, of inner liberty and creativity. Grant that feast, dance and play, song and sense of humor may be part of our grateful experience of your redemption at work.

Challenge
the Mass Media

With blunt frankness, Christ challenges the proud and incorrigible exploiters of all kinds....The virtue of frankness never raises the issue of whether our actions and words about the truth of salvation help or hurt us.The crucial point is always whether and how they promote the salvation of everyone.

The heavens are telling the glory of God; and the firmament proclaims his handiwork. Day to day pours forth speech, and night to night declares knowledge. There is no speech, nor are there words; their voice is not heard; yet their voice goes out through all the earth, and their words to the end of the world.

"For nothing is covered up that will not be uncovered, and nothing secret that will not become known. What I say to you in the dark, tell in the light; and what you hear whispered, proclaim from the housetops."

Psalm 19:1-4a; Matthew 10:26b-27

Few matters challenge Christian discernment and talent as much as does modern mass media. If Christians who excel in this field can transmit strong convictions, the art of dialogue, vigilance for the signs of the times, and discernment, they are the kind of people this world urgently needs today.

Mass media offer a unique opportunity for proclaiming the Good News literally "from the housetops"; think of all those satellite dishes! The potential of media is stupendous. It can remind us of our moral obligations to solve the urgent problems of our times. It can spread peace-fostering information; give voice to the voiceless; awaken people's consciences about the hungry, the exploited, the victims of catastrophes. It can be instrumental in organizing actions of solidarity from one end of the earth to the other.

On the other hand, there is nothing more dangerous than that same mass media in the hands of the unscrupulous enforcers of subversive ideologies, or exploiters of human passion, greed, and aggression. The infatuation of a great portion of the German population with Hitler exemplifies this, for it could hardly have been possible, without a shrewd use of the radio, to propagandize a people not yet prepared for discernment in its use. When Hitler came to power each family was offered a receiver at almost no cost.

My own father's reaction was sharp: "As long as this man is in power, no receiver will come into our house; I don't want his voice heard in our home!" A neighboring family, as devout and Church-oriented as ours, took the receiver. After a few years they had not, thank God, lost their faith, but their trust in the Church's leaders was undermined and many of Hitler's slogans had taken over a good part of their thinking and their language.

Some years later, in Russia, I found homes equipped with radio loudspeakers that could not be turned off, programs that could not be personally selected. They had been designed and placed there by the Stalinists. Both of these regimes threatened grave sanctions against anyone who would dare to listen to another country's radio, lest they absorb *its* "subversive" ideology.

Ways to Challenge

Development of the mass media is still bringing forth profound cultural and psychological changes. This is a field in which Christians should make their presence known. We have to be well informed about how media shapes human consciousness. Those who are interested in human development will use all possible means to influence the media in this regard. To do so, they must learn to judge their own reactions fairly and cultivate the virtue of discernment.

When the printing press appeared, some five hundred years ago, and began to exercise a growing influence on public opinion, the Church reacted one-sidedly, using all available means of control, censure, and sanction. This kind of repressive control over our modern mass media is absolutely impossible, and most people react negatively to such control systems. But responsible users of the media can praise good programs, recommend specific movies and plays, warn against error and decadence.

What really matters today is that all people grow in discernment and foster this in Church and society. This is a basic human principle. One-on-one promotion of good books, periodicals, movies, TV programs, and the like is a very effective means of fostering the good and increasing one's own competence in discernment. Shared efforts in such actions are especially effective. Then we can also more systematically and effectively face the evil, unmask deceptions and dangers, and warn against them.

Modern mass media provide a new opportunity for all social classes and all nations, and easier access to our common cultural heritage. But a concerted effort is needed to guarantee a certain moral and cultural level, to check the efforts of power cliques in their abuses of media, and to block effectively any kind of group monopoly. This is one of the most important fields for the exercise of the lay apostolate and the pursuit of professional excellence.

There lurks the serious danger of passive reception, exposing ourselves uncritically to a haphazard stream of news and entertainment without asking what good or harm is presented. Another danger is the exaggerated cult of the "stars" in the literary, entertainment, and sports worlds. This cult often leads to an imitation of those who least deserve it. Many people tend to accept opinions uncritically simply because they are uttered by a "star."

Other Means of Influence

Active participation in pertinent dialogue allows us to exercise a beneficial influence on public opinion rather than exposing ourselves defenselessly to all kinds of dubious influences. The simplest means of influence is our judicious choice of the products provided by multi-media power mongers. Through careful choices, we speak forcefully in the market itself. Another important means of influence are our letters to the editor or journalist or artist, especially when these present a competent expression given with a constructive attitude. It is not fitting to send only letters of censure and reproach.

Chronic complainers quickly lose any chance of being listened to or taken seriously. Positive appraisal, however, can be very effective.

The director of a broadcasting company once told me that good programming frequently has little chance of success because nobody requests it and nobody praises it. Many years ago, when I was still teaching in our seminary in Germany, I was visited by a friend of a famous entertainer who had died a few days before. He had come to bring to our students the entertainer's greetings, uttered from his deathbed. Some weeks previously, the students had written a collective letter to him, praising his combination of good taste, expertise, and propriety. His reaction had been one of great joy. He said: "During so many years of my career I never received any acknowledgment from any churchman; yet what these students of theology have praised in my work was my most serious concern during my whole life."

Families should give serious attention to TV programs, since this means inviting guests into their home and recommending them to their children. All family members should meet frequently, in a common effort to make good choices. Unfortunately, in many families the art of dialogue, and even common family prayer, have been silenced by a craving for ever-new programs which are received uncritically and passively.

Discipline Needed

Consumers of mass media need many forms of self-discipline. It is not sufficient to protect ourselves against vicious and noxious quality. Quantity, too, has to be examined. How much time is spent in watching TV, or playing computer or video games? How many frivolous impressions have been made? How much money is spent in operating the equipment? How much passivity is created in the children? Those who continue to overuse mass media, and react too passively to its influence, will become addicted consumers with no ability to assimilate the material presented. Such people gradually lose the contemplative dimensions of life. The art of dialogue becomes even more difficult and more rare.

This leads to yet another dimension of a much-needed form of self-discipline for those who expose themselves too often to publicity and advertisement. Media's mass message is: "Thou shall covet; thou shall buy more things; thou shall consume more...." We have to be on guard against the seductions of materialism and humanism.

Particularly dangerous is the intensive advertisement for psychotropic drugs. Drug addiction in our society is only the tip of the iceberg of an ever-growing tendency— propagated by the drug industry—to take pills instead of recognizing and organizing our own spiritual and psychological resources, living within our capacities, and cherishing healthier relationships with family, neighbors, and community.

Almost everyone today is either passively exposed to or has perceptively understood the pluralism of cultures and world views. The era of closed groups and cultures has ended. People are no longer guided by uniform traditions, customs, mores, world views, convictions. The media allows us to compare these dimensions in all their diversity.

This can be taken as a challenge to search more thoroughly for truth and solid moral convictions, and thereby to sink deeper roots into the community of faith.

There we find the most authentic help, especially when it fosters careful discernment and distinction between the abiding truth of divine revelation on the one hand, and changing human traditions and world views on the other.

The need for mature discernment is heightened by the fact that today's pluralism places constructive dialogue and peaceful discussion in competition with intolerant and aggressive ideologies, as well as economic and political systems whose weaponry is the ruthless manipulation of people's minds.

We must help each other to hold firmly to the abiding truths and principles of our faith, and to unmask dangerous errors. At the same time, we need to remain open to the great diversity of life expressions, which can be vital personifications of the one faith in various times and cultures. For this, too, the world needs persons who live the Gospel: mature and competent Christians.

The manner in which Christians are present in the world of media will determine how much influence they will have in deciding such burning questions of our day as the reconciliation of the Christian churches, and harmony and peace among nations.

Prayer

God, our Father, we adore you for the wonders of your revelation. We thank you for Christ, the great communicator on earth. We praise you for sending us the Spirit of Truth, enabling us to become attentive receivers and skillful and reverent communicators of truth.

We praise you, God, for having enabled men and women to more and more discover the secrets hidden in your creation, allowing them to communicate by new electronic technologies so that news can go from one end of the earth to the other in seconds. We are grateful for this progress in research which tells us of ever-new dimensions of the greatness of your creation.

We do believe, Lord, that it is your design to lead us all to you through your communication in creation and redemption. We thank you for the mass media, through which you invite the whole of humanity to a worldwide dialogue, new forms of solidarity, and new means of fostering peace. Help us, Lord, to reach that level of wisdom and discernment that allows us to make beneficial use of all these means.

Shape Public Opinion

I f we want to have a share in the Beatitudes, then we must also make a radical commitment to the demands that they make and keep pressing forward in the direction that they lead. We must avoid giving our allegiance to a watering down of virtue, a degradation that only deforms and discredits it.

Ah, you who drag iniquity along with cords of falsehood, who drag sin along as with cart ropes....Ah, you who call evil good and good evil, who put darkness for light and light for darkness, who put bitter for sweet and sweet for bitter! Ah, you who are wise in your own eyes, and shrewd in your own sight!

Isaiah 5:18,20-21

Since living a Christian life essentially means we're missioned to be "the light of the world," it is unthinkable that genuine Christians would ignore or neglect their responsibility for the formation of healthy public opinion in the surrounding environment and in society at large. A joint effort to enlighten and shape public opinion is a basic function of our care for the common good.

Of course, this does not mean merely theoretical opinions, which have no relevance for life, love, and justice in human relationships. Rather, it means those convictions and opinions that shape the human milieu: human encounter and cooperation, individual and collective responsibility.

Public Opinion

Some public opinion says:"Life is wonderful, a sign of God's creative presence. Human life, from the very beginning, is entrusted to the responsibility and protection of all. If society and state do not protect the life of the weakest and most innocent ones, the common good is shaken at its very foundations." But in some circles, public opinion may sound like this: "My body is mine. My womb is mine. It's nobody's business but mine if I choose to terminate my unwanted pregnancy."

In the economic realm, one camp of public opinion tells us: "What counts in the national economy is the quantitative growth of output. If a government fails in this area, it should be turned out." Others believe that the struggle for more and more output, and the tendency to measure prosperity and the common good by the quantitative national gross product, are grievous errors that can only lead to disastrous consequences for the future of humankind. If we do not free ourselves from this "more, more, bigger, bigger" madness, it will lead to worldwide conflict, even to ecological collapse.

A third example is equally pressing. Some insist on the right to health care for all. "The state and society have to do much more for health, and we have the right to get as much as possible from them and from our insurance policies." Others disagree. Certainly, the common good and justice require us to provide the best possible care for the sick, the handicapped, the poor. But the main efforts in public health care should be directed toward eliminating the common causes of sickness and disability: all forms of affliction that cripple persons, personalities, and human relationships. We must learn to accept responsibility for our own health and the health of others. We owe it to ourselves, to our families, and for the common good to promote health through our own healthy lifestyles.

Almost all the major decisions in our lives are programmed, somehow predetermined, by the quality of current public opinion. This is especially true in an age of democracy. Those who lack commitment to the formation of good public opinion demonstrate their neglect when they allow or request those in authority to pass laws and enforce measures which are clearly contradicted by a public-opinion majority.

However, we should not forget that legislative actions taken by administrators are also factors influencing public opinion, particularly if the legislators and administrators can give convincing reasons for their decisions. For them, too, the art of dialogue and an intelligent contribution to public opinion are decisive.

Freedom of Speech

The right to free public utterance of opinions and convictions, and to active participation in efforts to form public opinion, is a modern acquisition. Nations with right-wing dictators and communistic bureaucracies deny and oppose this right. Citizens in such countries have only the right to applaud the measures and ideologies of those in power. Transgressions are severely punished, and those who oppose the power cliques are heavily penalized.

But even in healthy democracies the right to free

speech has its limits. Freedom of speech is prohibited when the evident intention is the destruction of democracy, or public incitement to crimes against others. As Christians, we firmly approve freedom of speech within the indicated limits. Our assent presumes that we are willing to accept our shared responsibility in the search for healthy public opinion—and to acquire the necessary competence for that purpose—and that we tirelessly seek truth and justice.

In the past, secular and ecclesiastical authorities opposed freedom of public expression because of a deeply rooted pessimism about the good will and wisdom of the "ordinary people," while exhibiting a naive optimism about their own capacity to know what is right, true, and good. History plainly shows that powerful minorities excluded the powerless majorities from the truth-seeking and decision-making processes because of their own self interests and lust for greater power.

The Church's teaching authority has a special obligation to be a learning Church. Listening to the Word of God and proclaiming it cannot be dissociated from listening to people, especially to those of humble condition, of whom Jesus speaks in joyful prayer:"I thank you, Father, Lord of heaven and earth, because you have hidden these things from the wise and the intelligent and have revealed them to infants" (Luke 10:21b). To properly understand these words, we need to remember that, in Jesus' time, the religious rulers and the ruling class showed great contempt for the lower social classes, especially for the rural population. Yet, most of the prophets came from those parts of the nation.

Vatican II says explicitly that lay people participate in the prophetic mission of the Church, and it draws this important conclusion:"To the extent of their knowledge, competence or authority the laity are entitled, and indeed sometimes duty-bound, to express their opinion on matters which concern the good of the Church" (*Lumen Gentium,* "Dogmatic Constitution on the Church," 37). Even in matters of doctrines which allow no contradiction, not only ordained theologians, but also lay people, can make relevant contributions toward formulating these truths in ways that manifest their fruitfulness for life and make them more understandable for the various cultures and social classes.

In those questions whose answers are not found in divine revelation, all the people of God are to take an active part in the effort to make proper judgments and find appropriate solutions. The stream of information and competent knowledge flows in from all directions.

No authority has the right to veto the contributions of those who have special competence and valuable experience. We could cite the long debates about taking a moderate interest for capital loans (usury). For centuries, the Church simply reaffirmed the earlier formulations and definitions, while lay people and theologians pointed to the different situation in modern economy. In not accepting input from its people and theologians, the Church caused great losses and suffering. It also harmed its own credibility, in this and other matters.

Our Competence

Our sense of responsibility for searching out and propagating sound opinions goes hand in hand with a sharper awareness of the limits of our competence. If the subject matter concerns vital problems and interests, this does not mean that those who do not have outstanding competence have to be silent. Rather, all should strive to improve their competence. Ordinarily, the art of dialogue is the best method. Through it, we learn to distinguish between deeply rooted and mature convictions on the one hand and tentative opinions on the other. Sometimes our best contribution may be a well-formulated question rather than a daring thesis. The formulation and further discussion of precise questions will induce all participants to more serious reflection, including those who propose the questions.

In the propagation of public opinion, Christians should not think in terms of overcoming the opposition and being declared winners; rather, their purpose is to simply make their creative contribution in the search for truth and provide authentic solutions to vital problems. Those whose first impulse is to impose their opinions on others tend to practice manipulation or employ abusive tactics. We recognize them by their clever mixture of praise and blame, reward and punishment; they reveal themselves by their countless deceptive maneuvers. One of their most effective tools is the use of semantics.

"Through loyalty to conscience, Christians are joined to others in the search for truth and for the right solution to so many moral problems which arise both in the life of individuals and from social relationships" (*Gaudium et Spes,* "The Church in the Modern World," 16). Only in love and responsibility for the common good, for the well-being of others, and in absolute respect for every sincere conscience can we fulfill our role in this fundamental area. And only by developing our contemplative dimension in the light of God can we avoid the danger of becoming manipulated manipulators.

Prayer

Lord Jesus Christ, you tell us that we are "the light of the world." Help us to remember that we receive your light, and the mission to be light for others, only as a gratuitous gift from you. Teach us to abide by and walk in your light so that we may discern everything in the light of your love and truth.

Lord, we live in an ambiguous world which can easily seduce us unless we have made a firm choice to follow your light, a choice which we must gradually personify with our whole being. Lord, cleanse us, strengthen us, so that we may become more and more transparent; then your light can shine through us. Make us a radiant community of faith, hope, and love, zealous for your saving justice.

Help us to create a "divine milieu" within our world, so that we can work effectively for public opinion which favors justice, forgiveness and peace, truthfulness, and sobriety. Strengthen our desire to acquire the kind of motivation and competence that will allow us to exercise a healing influence on civic life through the formulation of good public opinion.

Maintain *the* Environment

At this moment, frugality has actually become a matter of survival....The once enormous supplies of nonrenewable resources are being used up with blinding speed. The by-products of our consumption crush the ecosystem; the earth's protective ozone layer has already been seriously eroded. How long will it be before our planet "runs out of breath"?

God created humankind in his image, in the image of God he created them; male and female he created them. God blessed them, and God said to them, "Be fruitful and multiply, and fill the earth and subdue it; and have dominion over the fish of the sea and over the birds of the air and over every living thing that moves upon the earth....See, I have given you every plant yielding seed that is upon the face of all the earth, and every tree with seed in its fruit; you shall have them for food. And to every beast of the earth, and to every bird of the air, and to everything that creeps on the earth, everything that has the breath of life, I have given every green plant for food." And it was so. God saw everything that he had made, and indeed, it was very good. And there was evening and there was morning, the sixth day.

And the LORD God planted a garden in Eden....Out of the ground the LORD God made to grow every tree that is pleasant to the sight and good for food, the tree of life also in the midst of the garden, and the tree of the knowledge of good and evil.

Genesis 1:27-31; 2:8a,9

The new world situation and new knowledge have brought ecology to the foreground of human and Christian responsibility. This is not to imply, however, that in this area we have nothing to learn from Christians of the past. Remember Saint Francis of Assisi and his loving respect for animals and plants, the sun and the moon. Saint Alphonsus' *The Art of Loving Jesus* relates how he admires our God for revealing divine beauty and goodness, and for speaking to us of God's own loving care for all of created reality.

The saints combine a spirit of praise and reverence for God's gifts with a temperance that prevents them from idolizing creatures or becoming slaves to them. This basic attitude is, in the long run, more effective than are mere principles and laws for the protection of ecological balance.

If the world of today would return to the spirit of praise found in the Bible and in all true disciples of Christ, it would not be too difficult to resolve the ecological crisis we speak of. Through these means we have been taught a redeemed and redeeming relationship with all of creation, together with a solidarity with all of humankind, in our own times and in generations to come.

The two accounts of creation in the first two chapters of Genesis are highly relevant for a right understanding of the relation between humankind and nature. Both accounts speak of God's loving care for privileged humans, but they also tell of God's joy in all created reality and solicitude for all living creatures. God has given us no right to feel entitled to exploit nature. God's will is that our attitude toward the environment be God's own attitude. As divine images, we want creation to be—and to remain—"very good."

By entrusting the wondrous Garden of Eden to our first parents, God does indeed show great confidence in us. If we entrust ourselves to God, and accept divine guidance to revere God in our celebration of the Sabbath and to continually worship our Creator in all our divine and human relationships, we surely will not lack a spirit of discernment and responsibility toward the environment. Some modern writers try to blame divinely inspired Scripture for our reckless treatment of the environment. To this end, they distort the word "subdue," taking it out of context and reading into the text an orientation toward a one-sided "doctrine of domination."

The prevailing "doctrine of domination" and the exploitation of nature in modern science, technology, economics, and politics are main causes of the sad ecological situation. Scripture favors a sensible attitude toward the material world, the plants and animals, and contributes partially to the development of modern science and technology in the Western World.

The God of the Bible is the Creator. God blesses the works of creation, and teaches humanity about the pre-eminence of saving truth and knowledge of salvation. This includes our responsibility for the wholeness of persons, for good human relationships, and care for a healthy world.

Even after the first sin, and later when the world was

flooded with sins and sinful ways, God took care of all the species of animals—the pure and the so-called "impure." In accord with the covenant with Noah, people are now entitled to eat the meat of animals—but only with the condition that they imitate God in the preservation of the animal world (see Genesis, chapters 7-9).

We Christians, who take seriously the mission that we are "the salt of the earth," need to properly inform ourselves about our complex ecological problems in order to exercise our influence responsibly, to make our contributions toward shaping public opinion and important political decisions in this area.

Qualities We Must Have

We must be adorers in spirit and truth, gifted with wisdom and discernment, and creative in an affirmative sense. This creativity allows for prudent manipulation of the given material of our environment. We do not encroach on the limits of our mandate to subdue the earth when we unfold the dynamics of biological and other processes, or when we use our knowledge and skill to transform them in ways that help many and harm none.

We could not have our gardens, our agriculture, our capacity to feed six billion people without selective breeding, without irrigating arid land. We do well to thin out the forests in proper proportion and to multiply the harvest by chemical fertilizer. We are worthy of praise when we lay out wonderful parks and gardens; for even after the Fall it remains true that God has entrusted the earth to us as a wonderful garden. God put Adam "in the garden of Eden to till it and keep it" (Genesis 2:15). Nothing can be said against our skill and planning in mining minerals used for the many purposes of economy and art. But all this has to be done with wisdom and care, so that the harmony of innumerable ecological factors which make for a healthy life will not be destroyed.

But today's highly developed scientific and technological people come ever closer to limits which may not be exceeded without endangering the earth. Irreversible mistakes can be made by unwise pioneering in an area where the complex interplay of various factors is not yet known to us.

The earth is part of an interaction between the sun and all the planets, and the solar system itself moves and develops in a not-yet well-known interplay with all the other factors of the universe. On earth, billions of factors in the most complex interplay constitute the biosphere, the milieu of human life.

This interaction has already been seriously disturbed by recent developments, for instance, the waste of irreplaceable minerals, especially fossil energy resources, and by pollution of water and air. Billions of fish, destined by the Creator to reproduce themselves for all generations, die because of water pollution resultant of various poisons from industrial wastes. The margin of tolerance of ionizing radiation by industry and armaments has been exceeded in many parts of the world. In spite of efforts for a worldwide ban, asbestos is still produced and used in increasing quantities, although it is now known as a principal cause of cancer.

The recent amazing progress in research of recombinant DNA might be a blessing in the field of medicine and genetics. It might open new horizons for selective breeding of plants, cereals, animals, and so on. But it might also produce irresistible viruses and endanger the genetic heritage.

Questions We Must Ask

The most threatening aspect in this whole situation is that today's world has invested its energies one-sidedly in the doctrine of domination and exploitation, while permitting itself a shocking lapse of development in wisdom and discernment. The highly developed technologies of countries in both the East and the West are the main causes of a disturbed biosphere and ecosphere. If the countries of the so-called Third World were to encourage the same quantitative growth mania and excessive waste in consumption and armaments, humanity would be close to a total ecological collapse.

The main culprits and profiteers in this picture of ecological damage are also the outspoken enemies of a worldwide effort to raise people's awareness of the situation and to form an ecological conscience. A host of scientists seem set on deceiving the people who are becoming aware of the grave ecological dangers. Yet, must not many of us ask ourselves, sincerely and humbly, if we are not somehow among the culprits? Are we ready to examine, and eventually to change, our consumer habits, our proneness to all kinds of waste? Have we that sound relationship with created reality which is based on adoration of God in spirit and truth? Are we willing to take our share of responsibility to promote a radical change of public opinion and lifestyle?

A new asceticism beckons us to a new kind of fasting, renunciation, and temperance as part of a lifestyle marked by simplicity and the joys inherent in it. When we seek and cultivate joy in God, the spirit of adoration and praise, the inner peace and charism of peacemakers; and when we cherish the final hope based on the divine promises and on the immense beauty we find in a healthy environment; and when we continue to pray more for wisdom than for success, power, and wealth—then we will no longer feel the need for so many things that our wasteful culture induces us to want. And when parents begin to give themselves and their genuine love to their children, they will no longer need to give them useless or unnecessary "things" as substitutes for their missing love. Thus our children, too, will develop in a healthier environment.

Prayer

Lord Jesus Christ, you came to earth to adore the Father in the name of all humanity and all creatures by the full truth of life, and thus to teach us "adoration in spirit and truth." Open our eyes, our hearts, and our minds to see the beauty and destiny of creation. You have taken the flesh of the earth to redeem the world. We want to thank you, by our lives, for having taught us to nurture healthy relationships among all people and to appreciate the gifts entrusted to our stewardship.

Help us, O Lord, to strive more for wisdom, knowledge of salvation, and discernment than for power and wealth. Help us to fulfill our firm purpose to administer our earthly heritage in solidarity with the poor and in responsibility for future generations.

Enlighten those who have special competence in problems concerning the human biosphere and ecosphere. Guide with your wisdom those who have to make grave decisions in economics and politics. Help them to face realistically all ecological problems and to resolve them wisely in cooperation with all people.

Lord, forgive us our sins against your creation, against the earth and the future generations; forgive our coveting more possessions, our mania for more consumption. And forgive us our cowardly silence in the face of all the dangerous delusions of our culture.

Promote Christian Culture

Thankful people store up in their grateful memory all the good experiences of the past. And in this way, the richness of the past, of tradition, and the whole variety of positive experiences, become a treasure, a source of energy for the here and now.

For it is as if a man, going on a journey, summoned his slaves and entrusted his property to them; to one he gave five talents, to another two, to another one, to each according to his ability. Then he went away. The one who had received the five talents went off at once and traded with them, and made five more talents. In the same way, the one who had the two talents made two more talents. But the one who had received the one talent went off and dug a hole in the ground and hid his master's money. After a long time the master of those slaves came and settled accounts with them. Then the one who had received the five talents came forward, bringing five more talents, saying, "Master, you handed over to me five talents; see, I have made five more talents." His master said to him, "Well done, good and trustworthy slave; you have been trustworthy in a few things, I will put you in charge of many things; enter into the joy of your master." Matthew 25:14-21

Our history as human beings flows from nature and culture. Essentially, we are cultural beings, enabled and enriched by culture and devoted to culture. Surely, then, all of us should invest the talents we have received from God and make them profitable for all by promoting a culture that favors healthy personal relationships, growth of creative liberty and fidelity, and arrangement of the environment that actualizes truth, goodness, and beauty.

Culture includes the shape of the landscape, the style of living, the decoration of the home. As we have just seen, one of the greatest achievements of culture is a responsible attitude toward the milieu, the whole arrangement of the environment in view of the health and wholeness of persons and communities.

The arrangement and development of economic structures, processes, and dynamics in view of justice and peace should be among our greatest skills, but we frequently fail because we lack a vision of wholeness which is the heart of all cultural endeavors. Christians who possess the vision of wholeness and the necessary qualities of character—as well as the necessary competence to serve the common good, justice, and peace—are surely among the faithful servants to whom the Lord and Giver of talents promises a place at the festive table when the great day of accounting has arrived.

Gratitude for Our Heritage

Our dedication to the promotion of culture in its various areas and dimensions should be an expression of gratitude for our God-given talents, our cultural inheritance, and our eagerness to serve present and future generations. Teachers of moral law, and all who want to fulfill their role in the ongoing history of salvation, have to be "like the master of a household who brings out of his treasure what is new and what is old"(Matthew 13:52b).

In the face of changing situations, needs, and possibilities, the outstanding moral and religious leaders—prophets and saints who discover new values or different ways to actualize traditional values—are those who are among the greatest promoters of culture. They do this by establishing a perfect balance between the old and the new. Their work in helping human persons to reach the peaks of human culture will stand as a priceless masterpiece.

When we consider the immense relevance of culture in all its dimensions, and when we recognize what it can do for the well-being and dignity of all men and women, each of us—in accord with our own capabilities—should give explicit attention to the promotion of culture so that its positive benefits are shared with all people, especially the poor.

In order to make a realistic contribution in this area, we need first to examine our society and its culture. Then we can try to discern what benefits human persons and healthy relationships, and what harms them. Our mission to be "the light of the world" and "the salt of the earth" will also demand our critical evaluation of the culture; as well as a diligent pursuit of the best possible ways to contribute to sound public opinion, which is such an important dimension of all cultures.

The Church and Culture

It is an undeniable fact that, in the course of history, religion has made great contributions to the promotion of culture in almost all fields. The cultural productiveness of faith depends very much on how much the joy of faith influences the work of genius. Believers' irreplaceable contributions are their vision of wholeness, vigilance for the signs of the times, and the convincing embodiment of faith in their daily lives.

One of the basic models for Christian involvement in culture is the Incarnation of the Word of God. Born an Israelite, Jesus the God-man grew up in that culture. He owed his range of thought, his use of language, and his vision of history to the traditions of his people. The best of that culture, marked by God-experience and by prophetic actualization, came to its fullness in him. Jesus did not originate all the religious and moral values that he lived and proclaimed in a totally new way. Rather, he incorporated all the treasures of the religious and moral culture of Israel into his own unique mission in the fullness of time.

Jesus did not allow the Jewish culture to monopolize his thinking. He often praised the faith of people who did not belong to that culture. Saint Paul explained this in view of the common calling of both Jews and Gentiles to the new covenant in Christ. Barriers created by mere people have to be removed in order that the good in all cultures can be appreciated and brought into this wholeness. "Whatever is true, whatever is honorable, whatever is just, whatever is pure, whatever is pleasing, whatever is commendable, if there is any excellence and if there is anything worthy of praise, think about these things" (Philippians 4:8).

Faithful to his mission, Paul could say: "I am a debtor both to Greeks and to barbarians, both to the wise and to the foolish" (Romans 1:14). Vatican II, in its treatment of newly established communities of the faithful, insists that the Church must be incarnated in the various cultures so that "the Christian life will be adapted to the mentality and character of each culture" (*Ad Gentes,* "The Church's Missionary Activity," 22). A constant effort to do likewise must also be made even in old established communities where a new culture is evolving. The spirit of evangelical poverty requires that we no longer cling to traditional forms where this would tarnish the newness of life in Christ and our mission to be "the salt of the earth."

If faith is deeply rooted in our hearts and minds, in faithful vigilance for the signs of the times we will use to the full our present opportunities to make our approach to various cultures and subcultures creative and redemptive. When we fully appreciate all the good in our own and other cultures, and when we blend this appreciation with our full vision of faith and wholeness, we become better able to face the blemishes of our own culture—to purify what needs to be purified, and to oppose what contradicts human dignity.

Prayer

We praise you, Lord of heaven and earth, for having given to humankind such admirable capacities to cultivate the earth, to till the garden you have entrusted to us, and to care for it. You have given skill to artisans and have gifted many with a sense of beauty in their pursuit of the higher arts. Song and music are your gifts and people's joy. Above all, we thank you for having called us all to be co-artists with you as we strive to become masterpieces of goodness, love, peace, wisdom, and beauty.

We thank you for the rich cultural heritage of our own nation and of all peoples, for the unique opportunity in our era when cultures can enrich each other and cultivate unity in variety as well as variety in unity. May all feel that gratitude can be best expressed by creative fidelity and responsibility in consideration for present and future generations.

Assist your Church throughout the world to remain faithful to the momentous occurrence of the first Pentecost, and to proclaim the Gospel in all languages to all cultures. Free Christians everywhere, especially in "powerful" nations, from all kinds of cultural "superiority" complexes. Lord, help us all to be faithful stewards in the promotion of Christian culture.

Transform *the* Economy

I nveterate selfishness...takes aim at the spirit....[and] is at work...in the very structure of modern life, for example, in the terrible fact that the 20 percent of humans inhabiting the Northern Hemisphere consume 80 percent of the nonrenewable resources while emitting 80 percent of the harmful pollutants, and, in the process, damaging our planet and our lives.

Make friends for yourselves by means of dishonest wealth so that when it is gone, they may welcome you into the eternal homes. Whoever is faithful in a very little is faithful also in much; and whoever is dishonest in a very little is dishonest also in much. If then you have not been faithful with the dishonest wealth, who will entrust to you the true riches? And if you have not been faithful with what belongs to another, who will give you what is your own? No slave can serve two masters; for a slave will either hate the one and love the other, or be devoted to the one and despise the other. You cannot serve God and wealth.

Luke 16:9-13

For today's Christians—more so than for the first generation of Christ's disciples—active participation in economics is imperative. This is clearly based on a fundamental option: Only by setting our minds completely on God's kingdom and God's saving justice can we arrive at true freedom in the economic realm and fulfill our liberating mission.

When we exercise our option to view economics under the banner of the Beatitudes, we gradually rid ourselves of blindness. We begin to realize how frequently and how easily economic success and power are leagued with "unjust mammon," with sinful economic structures and degrading exploitation and relationships.

We need to be leaders in the flight from all complicity with greed, and from the reckless striving for wealth and economic power that is so detrimental to so many people. Our flight, however, must not constitute a betrayal of our mission to be "the salt of the earth," and "salt" also to socioeconomic life.

Flight from greed and the idolatry of wrongful economic values frees us to participate in creative and constructive measures for improving the economy. This is a prerequisite for being "the light of the world."

We are reminded: "Be sure of this, that no fornicator or impure person, or one who is greedy (that is, an idolater), has any inheritance in the kingdom of Christ and of God" (Ephesians 5:5). We are as accountable for our sins of greed as for our sins of sexual indecency.

Modern Economic Systems

The modern development of economics is, from one point of view, a huge success. It manages to feed close to six billion people. Most citizens of highly industrialized nations live abundant lives. But modern economics has failed miserably in the matter of just distribution. Many millions of people live in misery, suffering starvation as Lazarus did at the threshold of the rich reveler. The sad reason is that, since the rise of capitalism, economic life is crowded with sinister idols and ideologies in both the East and the West.

For many people, economic activity is governed exclusively by motives of material success, efficiency, wealth, and power. Classical liberalism advanced an ideology that "justified" this approach while, at the same time, leaving the "successful" with a "good" conscience. It taught that the economic realm had to develop according to its own dynamics and incentives; it should not be harassed by moral imperatives. It promised that individualism would guarantee the best possible success and allow for the interplay of supply and demand.

Many who call themselves "Christian" have followed this reasoning. And if, by some chance, they become uneasy of conscience, they try to quiet and console it with almsgiving and pious or humanitarian philanthropies.

Marxism disapproves of individualism, not for moral reasons, but because of its attitude toward private property. It rejects the ethical foundation of socialism, since inherent to its ideology of socioeconomic life is class war and class hatred as the dynamic of historical development. In the existing systems of Marxism, the machinery of state-capitalism functions even more heartlessly than in capitalist systems with private ownership of productive capital.

Even with the bad effects of "unjust mammon," some important social advantages are made possible by the free enterprise system and by some socialist states. In many countries, insurance is available for times of illness and unemployment, and economic security is provided for workers after retirement. In some countries, employees have been given more say in the decision-making process and a better share in the business profits. Considerable—but still insufficient—efforts are being made to humanize labor.

Christians know from experience that the effects of original sin, "the sin of the world," are present in the economic realm. Economic greed has shaped harmful structures confirmed by no less harmful ideologies. Promoted through the powerful channels of mass media, bizarre "commandments" are being insinuated: Thou shalt covet; thou shalt buy more; thou shalt consume more; thou shalt flaunt thy wealth!

Jesus came to redeem all people, regardless of their ideologies. It therefore behooves us to encourage all efforts for more justice, unselfishness, moderation, and freedom from strife as signs of hope for redemption and liberation. We must directly oppose dangerous economic idols and ideologies, but at the same time we should keep our eyes and hearts open to welcome any efforts directed toward an authentic culture in the economic realm.

Empirical studies show the shocking extent of unethical and criminal conduct in business. Some managers and owners conduct their businesses on the basis of borderline morality—and then they consistently lower their standards. Powerful groups in industry and business use means—often unfair—to block legislation that would set a minimum of legally required standards of honesty and justice.

Too many of us do not trouble ourselves to act ethically. We can be "the salt of the earth" in the economic realm only when we are absolutely honest and reliable, even when this requires sacrifices and creates disadvantages.

Yet, in today's world, even this is not enough. Knowledge, competence, and cooperation are needed, as well as good will. For this purpose, we would do well to study the social doctrines of the Church and all other promising leads.

Our Christian Goals

These enormous tasks can be undertaken only by solidly united and competent Christians cooperating with all people of good will. There are some important goals to keep in mind.

- Application of the basic principles of social justice
- A worldwide solidarity, especially among all who participate in economic life
- Subsidiarity, which requires the highest possible level of sharing in decision-making processes concerning people's own well-being and the well-being of the powerless
- Justice to the aging and retired
- Effective application of equal dignity and equal rights for women in professional and industrial life
- Fair and generous cooperation between the highly industrialized wealthy countries and the poverty-stricken developing nations

Our call to salvation and holiness is essentially a call to mission, to *action.* Any who do not intend to cooperate in the salvation of all people, in all their dimensions and relationships—who do not accept their vocation to improve society as a whole—also destroy their own souls.

An affirmation of our co-responsibility for the improvement of community life, including the economic realm, is intimately connected with the decisive criteria which the Savior and Judge of the world indicated for the Day of Judgment (see Matthew 25:31-46). In working with others to improve community life, we capably perform the works of mercy and saving justice of which the Gospel speaks.

Private charity, important though it is, cannot substitute for a grave neglect of cooperation for a better ordering of the economic life, which in its present shape inflicts so many wounds, makes so many people lonely prisoners of "the system," submits countless people to hunger and starvation, and deprives many of decent care, clothing, and housing.

Our very lifestyle makes many of us a part of these unjust and harmful economic structures and activities. We need conversion. But individual conversion, which always takes precedence, implies more than personal disengagement. What is needed is that all the converted and all on the road to conversion work in solidarity for a profound change in our economic culture. We need to ask, of ourselves and of each other, questions like the following.

- Are we willing to free ourselves and others from the still-prevailing ideology of quantitative growth and to offer, instead, concrete and realistic—and, at the same time, idealistic—ways to qualitative growth?

- Are we willing to give concrete evidence that alternative ways of simple lifestyles are possible and even attractive?
- Are we willing to give personal witness that a moderate use of material goods brings more happiness and peace than wastefulness and greed?
- Are we willing to help each other to read the signs of the times, and to acknowledge that the present trend to ever-greater wastefulness of irreplaceable resources of energy and rare raw materials can no longer continue without grave injustice to future generations, indeed, even to our own generation?
- Are we willing to remind wealthy people and rich nations that the poorest people and nations have a legitimate claim to a rightful share of the earth's goods?
- Should we not combine the art of dialogue with convincing lifestyles so as to influence public opinion in this area?

We need a well-defined goal and a concerted effort to seek each day the proper means to establish a balanced socioeconomic order: an economy that serves real needs instead of creating artificial and harmful ones. We need to "beatitudinize" our economic system.

Beatitudes of Economy

Where people believe in the reign of God and concentrate on God's saving justice above all, there the weak and poor no longer are degraded and exploited.

*Where disciples of Christ hunger and thirst for
God's justice, there the greed for more money
and more power over others fades away.*

*Where believers practice Christ's gentleness, there
will be found a solution to conflicts.*

*Where people faithfully and gratefully praise the
God of mercy, there will be no class hatred, no
group selfishness, and no neglect of persons with
disabilities.*

*Where believers' hearts are purified by embracing
God's love, there will grow a sympathetic understanding of people's genuine needs.*

*Where men and women consider themselves highly
blessed and honored to be called children of God,
there will be total commitment to peace, justice,
and reconciliation.*

*Where people truly believe the message of the
Gospel, there will be brave souls who are ready
to suffer persecution and death for the sake of
authentic peace and saving justice. And despite
temporary lack of success, they will not lose
hope, for they have entrusted themselves to God.*

The message of the Sermon on the Mount, to "not
worry about your life, what you will eat or what you will
drink," and the invitation to "look at the birds of the
air...[and]...the lilies of the field," are in no way a call to
withdraw from public life and pursue our own selfish
interests. Rather, these words call us to the
all-encompassing mission to "strive first for the kingdom
of God" (see Matthew 6:25-34). Amazing things could
happen—economically, culturally, and politically—if we
would believe the Gospel with all our hearts.

Prayer

Lord Jesus Christ, you called yourself "bread for the life of the world." You lived and died for others, and you taught us to ask the Father for our daily bread, the bread which unites all people. Convert us, by the power of your Spirit, so that, as a community dedicated to mutual service, we may begin the task of arranging our socio-economic relationships in ways that respect the treasures of the earth and the fruit of our labor as gifts from the one God of us all.

Lord, deliver workers and business people from greed and division. Help us also to discover your design for salvation in the area of economics. Grant us wisdom and courage to work for the healing of economic structures that suffer from wounds of greed and lust for power. Give us saints who faithfully show us what it really means to believe in you as the Savior of the world.

Creator God, may the world perceive in us a people whose primary purpose is to honor your name, to pray for and to experience the coming of your reign. May we learn, from your generous and healing actions, to unite with others in efforts to remedy the appalling conditions that prevail on the world's economic front. Above all, renew our faith in your plentiful redemption, so that we will firmly commit ourselves to the liberation of all men and women from the enormous evils that beset our world.

Exert Political Influence

> In modern society, and particularly in modern political life, laws and regulations threaten to proliferate into infinity. As far as we can, we have to rein in this proliferation. In addition, we have to learn to distinguish where obedience is a genuine and necessary expression of communal responsibility and justice and where it would be out of place.

Jesus said... "Again it is written, 'Do not put the Lord your God to the test.'" Again, the devil took him to a very high mountain and showed him all the kingdoms of the world and their splendor; and he said to him, "All these I will give you, if you will fall down and worship me." Jesus said to him, "Away with you, Satan! for it is written, 'Worship the Lord your God, and serve only him.'" Then the devil left him, and suddenly angels came and waited on him.

Matthew 4:7-11

In the early Christian era, when a small minority of Christians could not even dream of exercising a positive influence in the political arena, simple people could do little more than quietly fulfill their civic duties and offer prayers "for kings and all who are in high positions, so that we may lead a quiet and peaceable life in all godliness and dignity" (1 Timothy 2:2). It was necessary that Christians be instructed on the meaning and limits of dutiful obedience to political rulers and civil laws. Only in their overall view do the texts of the Bible offer a fairly clear direction in politics. On the one hand, they affirm responsible obedience; on the other, they unmask and condemn abuse of political power.

The position of the early Church on political power was primarily critical. Jesus, himself *the* Prophet, continued and fulfilled the prophetic tradition which unmasked and chastised abuses of power and exploitation and oppression of the weak and poor. If Jesus had spoke only of the salvation of souls, the leaders of Israel and the Roman authorities would have left him in peace.

Jesus vents his prophetic wrath at the appalling abuse of religious authority displayed by the leaders of the Jewish people. He knows that he is to become a victim of their diabolical plot, arising from a mixture of religion and lust for power. His reaction to temptations (as recorded in Matthew 4:7-11) shows how shameless Jesus considers this kind of behavior and how sharply he opposes it.

As witnesses to the coming of God's kingdom, the disciples of Jesus are urged to develop attitudes directly opposed to those of the powerful people of this world (see Luke 22:24-27). If all Christians observed these directives, the great prophecies of the coming of God's reign would become more evident. The ongoing power struggles among us, and the insatiable hunger for privileges and noble titles, would finally be unmasked in their utter nonsense—all to the benefit of the political realm.

Human history is filled with erroneous and dangerous messianic expectations. With sadness, we recall the appalling theory of Pope Boniface VIII and others regarding the "two swords of the church"; all the "holy" wars; the wars of the Spanish crown against the South American Indians who were not ready to accept baptism; the wars of aggression waged by the early English Protestant colonizers against the North American aborigines. All these were based upon erroneous concepts of "chosenness" in preference to others.

History records numerous examples of this same sin of bias in the "secular" world: leaders who designated their states as "chosen nations" in the political and economic wars of Europe. American politicians who insisted on the "unconditional surrender" of Germans and Japanese during World War II, leading—in the latter case—to what was called "moral justification" for the use of atomic bombs against open cities in Japan. Apartheid politics in South Africa; "ethnic cleansing" in the former Yugoslavia; and Hitler's holocaust, an excuse for his myth of a "chosen" race.

Imperialism, militarism, and intolerance in their worst forms are the bitter fruits of various kinds of false religions and/or secularized ideologies of redemption.

Our Political Vocation

As true disciples of Christ, we know that when we think and speak of "chosenness" (election), which flows from our call to holiness and our mission to be "the light of the world," we do so only because we are humble followers of the Prince of Peace.

The frequently quoted and often misunderstood words of Jesus: "Give to the emperor the things that are the emperor's, and to God the things that are God's" (Matthew 22:21b; Mark 12:17a; Luke 20:25), means to steadfastly refuse to give the emperor divine worship, but to submit to his authority in other matters. All who pay to God what is due to God, adoring God throughout life (see Matthew 4:10), will contribute to the common welfare, but will never accord divine worship to sovereigns and states. New Testament texts that deal with political moral obligations have to be read within this context. If we follow the great prophetic tradition culminating in Christ, we will never be submissive followers of dictators, imperialists, or militarists. When Christians realize the importance of skillful participation in politics, and when we firmly believe in our vocation to holiness, the world will be blessed by men and women who are devout and competent political activists.

Scripture tells of the drastic tension between the original design of the Creator, the weakness of human nature after the fall from grace, and the fact of redemption. The decisive word is *redemption.* Believers, whose whole lives praise the gift of redemption, will discover the design of the Creator/Redeemer and will be able to face the reality of original sin, "the sin of the world." Power—especially absolute power—is exposed to the greatest temptations. History shows us that this is true.

Vatican II emphasizes the "otherness" of the apostles' successors. Their proclamation of the Gospel derives from "the power of God, who often shows forth the force of the Gospel in the weakness of its witnesses. Those who devote themselves to the ministry of God's word should employ the ways and means which are suited to the Gospel, which differ in many respects from those obtaining in the earthly city" (*Gaudium et Spes,* "The Church in the Modern World," 76).

Necessary Means for Political Renewal

The battle against individual and collective selfishness, and against the lust for power, goes hand in hand with a creative effort for political renewal. Our fight against personal sinfulness is inseparable from our fight against the "sin of the world," especially as it is manifested in abuses of power and authority.

An intelligent and faithful application of the principle of subsidiarity on all levels is one of the most effective means to establish a proper balance of power. This fundamental principle of Catholic social ethics implies a widespread and organic distribution of power whereby it is always subordinate to participation, service, and co-responsibility.

Individual initiative must not be hampered. What the family can do in a meaningful way should not be usurped by the political community. The purpose of family leadership is, above all, to strengthen the family's own functions. What can be done at the lower level should not be usurped by higher levels of political, social, or economic bodies. If urgent needs of the common welfare, or evident inability to perform the task, require higher authority to assume functions which would be performed ordinarily at a lower level, every effort must be made to restore conditions which will allow the lower level to perform the functions. All trends toward centralism must be considered abnormal at the very moment that they become opposed to subsidiarity.

When the principle of subsidiarity functions well on all levels—strengthening personal responsibility and guarding against appropriation of disproportionate power—we are able to favor and foster the development

of a world authority without the otherwise justified fear
that this might become perverted into an all-devouring
Moloch of power.

Democratic Process

The social doctrine of recent popes has favored a
spread of democracy insofar as this is historically possible. An authentic democracy is a federation-type orga-
nization that maintains a balanced distribution of power,
observance of the principle of subsidiarity, and election
(by the people) of representatives for only a specific
length of time. Free elections at regular intervals allow
the people to give approval or disapproval, to give
opportunities to other parties and coalitions, and to
indicate the main principles of the desired programs.

Democracy is built on a principle of tolerance and
free participation of all in the formation of public opinion.
A properly functioning democracy is unthinkable without the thorough political formation of all the people.
No party or government should be allowed a monopoly
in political formation.

Political formation involves the creation of a political
conscience. Citizens must know about the values at stake
in political decisions, and must follow a scale of values
by which to evaluate the decisions. A politically mature
conscience knows the proper goals of political activity.
There needs to be a constant effort for better political
achievement, and a readiness for self-criticism by the
individuals and groups involved. Yet, in striving toward
this ideal system, we must not forget that politics in an
imperfect and wayward world always requires the "art
of the possible."

When we vote, when we choose a particular political party, when we play our part in the formation of public opinion, we are constantly aware of the common welfare. We never lose sight of our political ideals. Realistically, there are times when we have to choose the lesser of two evils because the best is not available, but as long as we continue to work in the right direction, the "art of the possible" does not constitute a betrayal of conscience.

Prayer

Sovereign God, help us to perceive our political responsibility. Teach us to recognize that political formation is a duty we must not neglect. Grant us the gifts of wisdom and discernment. Free us from the bonds of narrowness, from the chains of collective and individual selfishness. Grant us, along with love for our homeland, a sense of global solidarity that prepares us to work with people all over the world.

Give us wise and competent men and women who have a genuine political vocation—people who are able to fulfill political roles in our communities, in our countries, and in international organizations.

Spread *the* Gospel *of* Peace

Unbounded love disdains the degrading recourse to violence. It is stronger than death. It conquers in suffering and even in death. And its victory is the healing, saving transformation of the enemy, the sinner. This powerful healing predicated on nonviolence is the gift in which Jesus wants us to share.

"Come, let us go up to the mountain of the LORD, to the house of the God of Jacob; that he may teach us his ways and that we may walk in his paths." For out of Zion shall go forth instruction, and the word of the LORD from Jerusalem. He shall judge between the nations, and shall arbitrate for many peoples; they shall beat their swords into plowshares, and their spears into pruning hooks; nation shall not lift up sword against nation, neither shall they learn war any more.

Isaiah 2:3-4

"Salt is good; but if salt has lost its saltiness, how can you season it? Have salt in yourselves, and be at peace with one another" (Mark 9:50). To "have salt in" ourselves means that we are permeated with the peace of the Lord. If we, whether individually or communally, lack peace, our Christianity is without flavor. The peace for which Christ came, and which he has promised to his disciples, is a blessed gift to everyone who truly believes in him and trusts in him. All who receive this gift gratefully realize that it is a gift intended for everyone: no one can be a possessor of peace without also being its messenger.

Jesus' Peace Mission

Peace is the pivotal point of the prophetic expectation of Israel, especially in the New Testament, which frequently is called "the Gospel of Peace." The *"Shalom"* of the risen Christ lifts his disciples from sadness and fills their hearts with joy and trust. And when he repeats his greeting, using the same word, he gives them their mission of peace: "As the Father has sent me, so I send you" (John 20:21). He breathes his peace into their hearts and grants them his Spirit whose fruits are "love, joy, and peace" (see Galatians 5:22).

An essential part of the peace mission is the proclamation of forgiveness to all who need it (see John 20:23). The apostles of peace and reconciliation come as Christ's ambassadors (see 2 Corinthians 5:20), pleading for people to heed the hour of favor. Jesus himself said that peacemakers will be called the sons and daughters of God (see Matthew 5:9).

Christ, as is evident from Scripture, wants to make sure that his disciples are able to distinguish true peace— granted by him—from all false talk about peace. Those who bring peace *do* disturb people: rousing their consciences, making them aware that they are in need of proper reconciliation and genuine peace. This detachment from false and even unworthy peace was strongly symbolized in Jesus' actions when he drove from the

Temple those who would make religion a business (see Mark 11:15-17).

We who desire the peace of Christ must separate ourselves from any spirit of deception, greed, or lust for power. Christ knows that his message will bring him anguish (see Luke 12:50). His person and his message force people to make decisions that will be violently opposed by those who reject his peace (see Luke 12:51-53). The messengers of Christ's Gospel of peace will experience what the prophet Simeon foretold at Christ's coming into the world: "This child is destined for the falling and the rising of many in Israel, and to be a sign that will be opposed so that the inner thoughts of many will be revealed" (Luke 2:34b-35a).

The Prince of the messianic peace, exalted on the cross, wants to draw people to himself and to God's kingdom by the power of his nonviolent love. This divine design of peace and salvation is a kind of two-edged sword. It forces our hearts to take sides: Are we *for* or *against* this peace?

Obviously, there were people in our Lord's time who misunderstood some of his words and actions. Jesus did not want his disciples to use the sword (see Matthew 26:52). Yet, earlier in Matthew (10:34) Jesus says, "Do not think that I have come to bring peace to the earth; I have not come to bring peace, but a sword." Luke is more precise: "Do you think that I have come to bring peace to the earth? No, I tell you, but rather division!" (Luke 12:51). Challenged by Christ, who is Peace in person, the hidden conflicts between light and darkness come into the open.

Those who still think that swords—or nuclear weapons—are the proper means for the reign of light should remember Jesus' abrupt response—"It is enough" (Luke 22:38b)—to his disciples' talk about swords. It is shocking to hear how often people who call themselves Christians continue to talk quite readily about the "two swords," confusing the sword of the Word of God with the weaponry of unredeemed humanity.

Our Peace Mission

We need to be ready and eager to resolve conflicts by nonviolent means. This is a part of our mission which we dare not decline. Do we *really* want to follow Christ in his courageous unmasking of hypocrisy and injustice? Then we must learn from him to suffer patiently and to forgive untiringly in our efforts to bring justice, truth, and peace to a world violently opposed to pacifism.

Mahatma Gandhi and Martin Luther King, Jr. risked their lives, and ultimately sacrificed them, for *satyagraha*, a system of nonviolence which emphasizes the power of truth, love, justice, and solidarity in the service of the downtrodden. Gandhi, though not formally a Christian, was a fervent disciple of Christ; he was convinced that this method embodies the central message of the Sermon on the Mount and the life and death of Christ.

In their *ashrams* (houses of prayer), the followers of Gandhi are trained in the use of *satyagraha*. They learn that it means nothing less than total dedication to the liberating truth that God is love and a God of peace. They are confident that this liberating truth, when totally upheld throughout life, is more powerful than all the onslaughts of evil.

This Ghandian method of achieving social and political reform relies on the art of detecting our inner forces of truth and love for ourselves and others (including our enemies), of regarding them as precious gifts of God, and activating them by unwavering love.

At this moment in history, when all the world has to choose between the dove of peace and the hawk of war, each family, each monastery, each parish, indeed the whole Church, should become an *ashram*—a house of prayer—wherein we allow the Divine Master to teach us, from within, the liberating truth of the power of the Gospel of peace. We need such houses of prayer, where we can learn the art of healthy and healing relationships, of peaceful solution of conflicts. Only after constantly imploring this gift of peace from above will it take root in the hearts of all.

Importance of Nonviolence

The only way we can break out of the vicious circle of the armaments race is for all of us to take on the attitude of and apply the skill of *satyagraha*. This will be a concrete sign of our faith in the Gospel of peace, and it should become the most effective "defense contract" we ever make. It will be the "armor of God." It will serve as our defense "against the rulers, against the authorities, against the cosmic powers of this present darkness." Using God's armor, we must put on the "belt of truth," make morality our "breastplate of righteousness," the Gospel of peace the "shoes for our feet." Then we will meet the world with "the shield of faith…the helmet of salvation, and the sword of the Spirit, which is the word of God" (see Ephesians 6:10-17).

Any nation or system of government that still clings to the awful madness of imposing its will and collective selfishness on other systems and nations, by brutal threats of nuclear and chemical warfare, must be brought to its senses and convinced of its wrong by communities and nations who have taken up the nonviolent weaponry of *satyagraha.* To heal those nations whose ills are caused by their ruthless ideologies, we need nations willing to withstand evil and solidly unite in the spirit and art of nonviolence.

In today's world, this method of nonviolence is perhaps the best way we can give witness to our faith in Christ, the Prince of Peace. Christians must make a conscious effort to utilize this gift of Christ. All people who have the inner strength to choose *satyagraha* and the sacrifices entailed are sons and daughters of God.

If humanity is to be saved from self-destruction, we must give witness to the Gospel of peace by our lifestyles, our love for one another, our attitude toward God's creatures, our wise and tolerant treatment of the ecology, our commitment to a qualitative (rather than a mere quantitative) growth of economic life, and our political efforts to ensure the reign of peace.

Mere passive pacifism, which stands clear of political controversy and other realities, will not do. As blessed peacemakers (Matthew 5:9), we must face the realities of life—right on the front line—in order to work for peace in a nonviolent way. As servants of peace, we must be ready to give our all, without complaining and without losing our faith in the Gospel of peace.

While it is infallibly true that God desires all humankind to pursue the goal of the Gospel of peace, we all are indeed fallible in the choice of steps we take in trying to solve or prevent conflicts on the road to final peace. But we must have this conviction about peace. Only then can we make progress in our quest for more justice and a more solidly grounded peace.

Prayer

God of peace, we bless you for not abandoning a rebellious and war-prone world in its alienation and self-destructiveness. We thank you for sending us your Son as Reconciler and Peacemaker. He has shown us the ways of peace and sealed his Gospel of peace by his precious blood.

Send forth your Spirit, so that we and all the world will understand how horrible is the fate which threatens humankind at this point in time. Bestow on us the fruits of the Spirit: truth, love, peace, and justice. Let your Spirit guide us on the path of peace.

Holy Spirit, help us to discover our inner resources for peace, which are your gifts to us. Activate these forces within us so that we may be credible witnesses for the Gospel of peace and the power of nonviolent action. Teach us to patiently and skillfully convince all of humanity that conversion to peace is most urgent in view of the threatening power blocks and dangerous ideologies which still dare to glorify violence, hatred, and claims of superiority in weapons of cruelty and destruction.

Lord, gird us with the weapons of love and peace, with invincible faith in the final victory of truth and love. Grant us the courage to commit ourselves to the Gospel of peace, whatever may be the necessary sacrifices. Let the Gospel of peace be "the shoes on our feet" to give us firm footing. May the power of your Spirit strengthen our faith as we strive for universal peace.